CROSSWORD PUZZLE
FOR A PLAN FOR MY FUTURE

Name : _____

Date : _

I0539856

Across

1: AN OPPORTUNITY TO REFLECT ON AND EVALUATE YOUR OWN WORK.

3: SENSE OF DIRECTION OR MEANING IN LIFE.

6: FEELING OF FELLOWSHIP WITH OTHERS, AS A RESULT OF SHARING COMMON ATTITUDES, INTERESTS, AND GOALS.

7: OUTLINING KEY MILESTONES AND EVENTS IN YOUR EDUCATIONAL JOURNEY. THIS CAN HELP YOU STAY ORGANIZED, TRACK PROGRESS, AND ENSURE THAT YOU MEET IMPORTANT DEADLINES.

9: PROCESS OF SELECTING A ORGANIZATION OR ESTABLISHMENT THAT ALIGNS WITH YOUR NEEDS AND GOALS.

10: CRUCIAL PROCESS FOR PERSONAL DEVELOPMENT AND ACHIEVEMENT.

Down

1: TO CONTACT SOMEONE FOR HELP OR ADVICE.

2: STRIVES TO DO WHAT'S RIGHT AND TO CARRY OUT DUTIES.

4: A CONNECTION BETWEEN PEOPLE.

5: DEDICATION AND LOYALTY ONE HAS TOWARD A PARTICULAR GOAL, RELATIONSHIP, CAUSE, OR RESPONSIBILITY.

8: THE ABILITY TO BE EMOTIONALLY STABLE, RESILIENT, AND LESS PRONE TO EXPERIENCING NEGATIVE EMOTIONS.

TABLE OF CONTENTS

CHAPTER 1
SELF ASSESSMENT

These questions are to encourage reflection and provide insights into areas where you can focus on improving yourself. Self-assessment is an ongoing process, so revisiting these questions regularly can help track your progress and make necessary adjustments in your personal and professional life.

Question:	Your Answer:
1. What things did I do this year that made me really proud?	
2. What am I best at? How have these skills helped me succeed?	
3. Did I achieve the goals I wanted? If not, what made it hard to reach them ?	
4. What were the hardest things I had to doal with ? How did I manage them, and what did I learn?	

Question:	Your Answer:
5. I am often the one to suggest activities with friends?	
6. What activities do I enjoy the most ?	
7. What do I think is most important in my life and in my work?	
8. Do I find it easy to make new friends and build relationships?	

A PLAN FOR MY FUTURE

MON   TUE   WED   THU   FRI   SAT   SUN

○   ○   ○   ○   ○   ○   ○

DATE: _____

CHAPTER 1
SELF ASSESSMENT

9. I define love as?

10. Have I been feeling really stressed?

"Write Your Thoughts"

A PLAN FOR MY FUTURE

MON   TUE   WED   THU   FRI   SAT   SUN
○   ○   ○   ○   ○   ○   ○

DATE: _____

CHAPTER 2
RELATIONSHIP AND COMMUNITY

These questions can provide insights into the strength, effectiveness, and impact of someone's support system, highlighting both the strengths and areas for improvement in the network of relationships and community connections.

Question:	Your Answer:
1. How can I meet more people to learn new things and find better jobs?	
2. Do I do things in groups like attending church or in a club? What is good about being in this group?	
3. What can I do to make sure things that upset me happens less?	
4. Are there people or places that help when things are tough?	

Question:	Your Answer:
5. Who do I feel closest to?	
6. Are there teachers who help me learn new things?	
7. Do I feel like I belong in my community?	
8. What do I like most about my friends?	

A PLAN FOR MY FUTURE

MON   TUE   WED   THU   FRI   SAT   SUN

○   ○   ○   ○   ○   ○   ○

DATE: _____

CHAPTER 2
RELATIONSHIP AND
COMMUNITY

9. Do I ever feel alone or like no one is there to help?

10. Who can I trust to help when something bad happens?

"Write Your Thoughts"

A PLAN FOR MY FUTURE

MON   TUE   WED   THU   FRI   SAT   SUN
○   ○   ○   ○   ○   ○   ○

DATE: _____

CHAPTER 3
CONSCIENTIOUSNESS

These questions are to help understand the role of conscientiousness in success: By answering these questions, readers can cultivate the qualities that lead to greater productivity, reliability, and long-term achievement.

Question:	Your Answer:
1. Do I plan my activities well in advance?	
2. How often do I create to-do lists or schedules?	
3. Is my workspace typically neat and organized?	
4. How important is it to me to be on time for appointments or meetings?	

Question:	Your Answer:
5. Do I prefer to arrive early or just in time for events?	
6. Do I often find myself striving for perfection at work or on tasks?	
7. How do I react when things do not go according to plan?	
8. Am I someone others can depend on to follow through on commitments?	

A PLAN FOR MY FUTURE

MON   TUE   WED   THU   FRI   SAT   SUN

○   ○   ○   ○   ○   ○   ○

DATE: _____

CHAPTER 3
CONSCIENTIOUSNESS

9. How good am I at sticking to long-term goals or plans?

10. Do I find it easy to motivate myself to complete tasks even when they are challenging or boring?

"Write Your Thoughts"

A PLAN FOR MY FUTURE

MON   TUE   WED   THU   FRI   SAT   SUN
 ○   ○   ○   ○   ○   ○   ○

DATE: _____

CHAPTER 4
ANXIETY

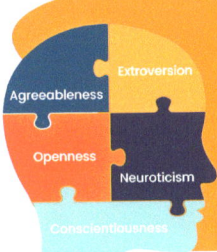

These questions are to guide individuals in recognizing how emotional instability affects their well-being. Addressing these questions helps readers manage anxiety, stress, and emotional challenges, leading to improved mental resilience and healthier decision-making.

Question:	Your Answer:
1. Do I worry about things that might go wrong?	
2. Do I find it difficult to bounce back quickly after experiencing a setback or disappointment?	
3. Do I find it challenging to control my emotions?	
4. Do I often blame myself or feel guilty, even when things are not entirely my fault?	

Question:	Your Answer:
5. Am I critical of my own performance and achievements?	
6. Do I dwell on past mistakes or failures?	
7. Do I frequently feel stressed or overwhelmed by responsibilities?	
8. Do I struggle to relax and unwind, even during vacation?	

A PLAN FOR MY FUTURE

MON   TUE   WED   THU   FRI   SAT   SUN

○   ○   ○   ○   ○   ○   ○

DATE: _____

CHAPTER 4
ANXIETY

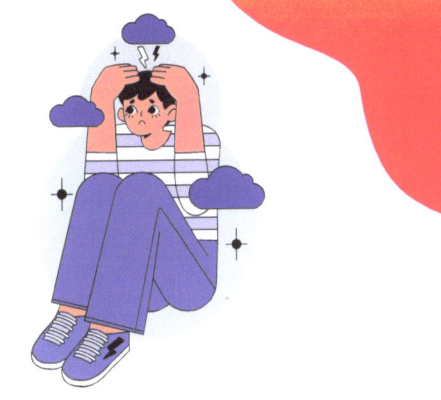

9. Do I take criticism or negative feedback personally?

10. Am I easily hurt by others' comments or actions?

"**Write Your Thoughts**"

A PLAN FOR MY FUTURE

MON   TUE   WED   THU   FRI   SAT   SUN

○   ○   ○   ○   ○   ○   ○

DATE: _____

CHAPTER 5
COMMITMENT

These questions are to reinforce the importance of staying dedicated to goals. By exploring these questions, readers can strengthen their resolve and perseverance, enabling them to overcome challenges and stay focused on long-term objectives.

Question:	Your Answer:
1. Do I feel a sense of determination and focus when working towards achieving my goals?	
2. Am I willing to make sacrifices or endure challenges to stay on track with my objectives?	
3. Do I view challenges as opportunities for growth rather than a reason to give up?	
4. Do I follow through on promises or obligations, even when it requires extra effort or sacrifice?	

Question:	Your Answer:
5. Do others rely on me to consistently to deliver high-quality work or support?	
6. Am I willing to invest considerable time and effort into tasks or projects that are important to me?	
7. Do I manage my time effectively to balance various commitments without compromising on quality?	
8. Do I demonstrate commitment and loyalty in my personal relationships, such as friendships or partnerships?	

A PLAN FOR MY FUTURE

MON   TUE   WED   THU   FRI   SAT   SUN

○   ○   ○   ○   ○   ○   ○

DATE: _____

CHAPTER 5
COMMITMENT

9. Am I dedicated to nurturing and maintaining meaningful connections with others over time?

10. Do I prioritize the wellbeing and happiness of those I care about?

"Write Your Thoughts"

A PLAN FOR MY FUTURE

MON   TUE   WED   THU   FRI   SAT   SUN

○   ○   ○   ○   ○   ○   ○

DATE: _____

CHAPTER 6

PURPOSE

These questions are to encourage reflection on life's deeper meaning. By answering these questions, individuals discover their purpose, leading to a more fulfilling and motivated life as they pursue goals that resonate with their true passions.

Question:	Your Answer:
1. What do I value?	
2. How do my values contribute to my sense of purpose and meaning in life?	
3. What are my long-term goals and aspirations?	
4. Do my goals align with my personal values and reflect what is meaningful to me?	

Question:	Your Answer:
5. How do my actions or contributions make a positive difference in the world or in the lives of others?	
6. Have I made an impact to my community, society, or environment? How?	
7. How do my relationships and connections with others contribute to my sense of purpose?	
8. Do I find fulfillment in sharing experiences, values, and goals with like minded individuals or communities?	

A PLAN FOR MY FUTURE

MON   TUE   WED   THU   FRI   SAT   SUN

◯   ◯   ◯   ◯   ◯   ◯   ◯

DATE: _____

CHAPTER 6
PURPOSE

9. How often do I reflect on the meaning and purpose of my life and actions?

10. Do I seek clarity and direction through introspection, mindfulness, or spiritual practices?

"Write Your Thoughts"

A PLAN FOR MY FUTURE

DATE: _____

CHAPTER 7
SETTING GOALS

These questions are to help readers clarify their aspirations. By answering these questions, individuals can break down their larger ambitions into achievable steps, track their progress, and stay motivated, ensuring a higher likelihood of success.

Question:	Your Answer:
1. Write a brief statement describing your ideal future.	
2. What do I hope to achieve or accomplish?	
3. What does success look like for me?	
4. My short-term goals are?	

Question:	Your Answer:
5. What specific roles or positions am I interested in?	
6. How does my career align with my personal goals and values?	
7. How do I feel about my future?	
8. How will my decisions affect my mental and emotional wellbeing?	

A PLAN FOR MY FUTURE

MON   TUE   WED   THU   FRI   SAT   SUN
○   ○   ○   ○   ○   ○   ○

DATE: _____

CHAPTER 7
SETTING GOALS

9. Outline the steps you need to take to achieve your goals. Break them down into smaller, more manageable tasks or milestones.

10. List the actions I plan to take in the near future to progress towards my medium and long-term goals.

"**"Write Your Thoughts"**

A PLAN FOR MY FUTURE

MON   TUE   WED   THU   FRI   SAT   SUN
○   ○   ○   ○   ○   ○   ○

DATE: _____

CHAPTER 8
SEEKING GUIDANCE

These questions are to highlight the value of mentorship and advice. Addressing these questions opens the door to valuable support and insights, helping readers make informed decisions, avoid pitfalls, and accelerate their personal growth.

Question:	Your Answer:
1. Who are the mentors or advisors I admire and why?	
2. What specific advice am I seeking right now?	
3. Are there challenges or decisions I need guidance on?	
4. Can I describe a situation where seeking guidance helped me make a better decision?	

Question:	Your Answer:
5. Are there professional networks or communities I turn to for advice?	
6. How do I evaluate the credibility and relevance of the guidance I receive?	
7. Have I considered formal mentoring programs or informal mentorship arrangements?	
8. What steps am I taking to build and maintain relationships with mentors or advisors?	

A PLAN FOR MY FUTURE

MON   TUE   WED   THU   FRI   SAT   SUN

○   ○   ○   ○   ○   ○   ○

DATE: _____

CHAPTER 8
SEEKING GUIDANCE

9. What steps am I taking to build a strong professional network that can offer learning opportunities?

10. Have I explored shadowing or mentoring opportunities to gain experience from experienced professionals?

"Write Your Thoughts"

A PLAN FOR MY FUTURE

MON   TUE   WED   THU   FRI   SAT   SUN

○   ○   ○   ○   ○   ○   ○

DATE: _____

CHAPTER 9
EDUCATION PATHWAY

These questions are to assist in making an informed decision about education. By asking these questions, readers can evaluate schools or universities based on their values and objectives, ensuring a choice that supports their aspirations.

Question:	Your Answer:
1. How does this institution help me achieve my academic, career, or personal goals?	
2. Do they align with my interests and intended areas of study or focus?	
3. Can I afford tuition, fees, and other expenses associated with attending this institution?	
4. Does the institution offer resources such as academic advising, career counseling, or student support?	

Question:	Your Answer:
5. Will I have access to personalized attention and mentorship?	
6. Is it a place where I can thrive academically, socially, and personally?	
7. Are there clubs, organizations, or events that align with my interests?	
8. Can I find reviews or testimonials that provide insights into student satisfaction?	

A PLAN FOR MY FUTURE

MON   TUE   WED   THU   FRI   SAT   SUN

○   ○   ○   ○   ○   ○   ○

DATE: _____

CHAPTER 9
EDUCATION PATHWAY

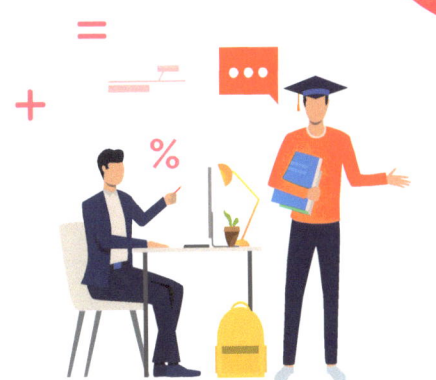

9. What is the institution's accreditation status?

10. What are the career outcomes for graduates of this institution?

"Write Your Thoughts"

A PLAN FOR MY FUTURE

MON   TUE   WED   THU   FRI   SAT   SUN

○   ○   ○   ○   ○   ○   ○

DATE: _____

CHAPTER 10
EDUCATIONAL TIMELINE

These questions are to encourage thoughtful planning of one's academic journey. By answering these questions, readers develop a structured plan that balances academic milestones with personal growth, helping them stay on track and achieve their desired outcomes.

Question:	Your Answer:
1. What degrees, certifications, or qualifications do I aim to achieve?	
2. When do I plan to start and finish each level of education or training?	
3. Have I completed all necessary steps to qualify for entry into my desire programs?	
4. How do I balance my academic workload with other responsibilities?	

Question:	Your Answer:
5. Can I realistically manage my studies alongside work, family commitments, or other activities?	
6. Do I need to plan for semester breaks, vacations, or time off to recharge?	
7. Do I require tutoring, mentoring, or additional study materials?	
8. Have I explored scholarships, financial aid options, or savings plans?	

A PLAN FOR MY FUTURE

MON   TUE   WED   THU   FRI   SAT   SUN

○   ○   ○   ○   ○   ○   ○

DATE: _____

CHAPTER 10
EDUCATIONAL TIMELINE

9. Do I need to consider internships, co-op programs, or practical experiences?

10. Have I researched potential career paths or industries related to my field of study?

"**"Write Your Thoughts"**

A PLAN FOR MY FUTURE

MON   TUE   WED   THU   FRI   SAT   SUN

○   ○   ○   ○   ○   ○   ○

DATE: _____

CROSSWORD PUZZLE FOR A PLAN FOR MY FUTURE

Name : _____

Date : _____

Crossword grid answers:

- 1 Across: SELF ASSESSMENT
- 3 Across: PURPOSE
- 6 Across: COMMUNITY
- 7 Across: EDUCATIONAL TIMELINE
- 9 Across: EDUCATION PATHWAY
- 10 Across: SETTING GOALS
- 1 Down: SEEKING GUIDANCE
- 2 Down: CONSCIENTIOUSNESS
- 4 Down: RELATIONSHIP
- 5 Down: COMMITMENT
- 8 Down: ANXIETY

ANSWER KEY WORKSHEET

ACROSS

1: SELF ASSESSMENT

3: PURPOSE

6: COMMUNITY

7: EDUCATIONAL TIMELINE

9: EDUCATION PATHWAY

10: SETTING GOALS

DOWN

1: SEEKING GUIDANCE

2: CONSCIENTIOUSNESS

4: RELATIONSHIP

5: COMMITMENT

8: ANXIETY

ALL ABOUT ME!

Facts About Me

Name _____

Age _____

Grade _____

Teacher _____

My Hero

_____

_____

_____

My Favorite Book

_____

_____

_____

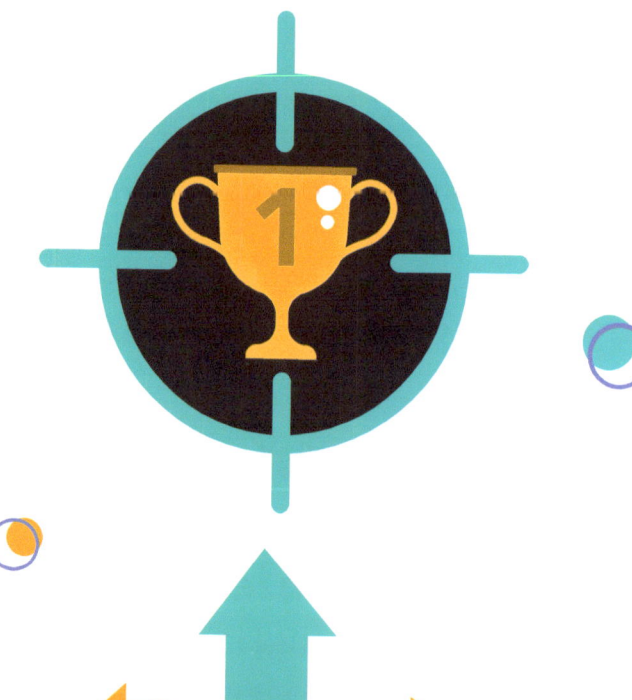